LIVING INSIDE
HIS CLOSET

LIVING INSIDE HIS CLOSET

Augie Mikesell

iUniverse, Inc.
New York Lincoln Shanghai

LIVING INSIDE HIS CLOSET

iUniverse books may be ordered through booksellers or by contacting:

iUniverse
2021 Pine Lake Road, Suite 100
Lincoln, NE 68512
www.iuniverse.com
1-800-Authors (1-800-288-4677)

ISBN-13: 978-0-595-37096-2 (pbk)
ISBN-13: 978-0-595-81497-8 (ebk)
ISBN-10: 0-595-37096-9 (pbk)
ISBN-10: 0-595-81497-2 (ebk)

Printed in the United States of America

I will always love my husband and though the story I am about to share with you, is true. I am writing this with hope of helping others like me see what I could not see...

Even though my husband has given his whole
life to others outside of the marriage, I did not
approve of his actions. I was raised in the
church even from the cradle and I felt this in
my heart. Noted in the Holy Bible. Romans
1:27 And likewise also the men, leaving the
natural use of a women, burned in their lust
one toward another; men with men working
that which is unseemly, and receiving in them-
selves that recompense of their error which
was met.

I hope this will help anyone that might be in the same position as I am, and give them hope or the courage to start the new life that I never did.

This is also dedicated to all the women that have a similar story, and my best friend Rhoda, who gave me the courage to tell my story and her friend Colette. May God Bless.

CONTENTS

PART ONE

I was fourteen and had been without a dad for five years. My dad passed away in September of 1962 at a young age of forty. My dad was always giving me a lot of attention and called me his princess and made me feel good about myself. He had what was called nephritis, which no one even told me about. I didn't know till the doctor came to the house one day and called for an ambulance that my dad was so ill. The ambulance came to take my dad and I wanted to go with him. The last words I heard from his mouth was "No honey, I'll be back." I never saw him alive again as he went into a coma and died. I guess mom felt I was too young to understand his situation, but I wish someone had warned me.

Now mom on the other hand, had been a moody person, taking Valium or Mother's little helper. She didn't do things like my dad did he was the greatest. Mom hardly ever hugged me or kissed me, or said anything positive to me. It was as if she resented me. Mom had been dating since dads passing and she found a husband after dating several gentlemen. I didn't like the most of them anyway. This new one was a bit different and he lost his wife to a suicide after she lost her precious son.

So I became a Step Daughter of a minister in the heart of Indiana when mom remarried at age forty-seven.

I gained a stepsister that was fifteen years old at the time and she and I learned to get along very well. We were instantly placed together in the same room to share a double bed and a new life together as sisters.

Then there was my little brother that was nine and a troublemaker for my sister and I. He has always been the baby of my family and the youngest always gets his older siblings in trouble. He of course got his own room where we all had to share the same small bathroom in the upstairs part of the large Victorian house.

My sister, I found out had a boyfriend down the street and I thought I should have one also, even though I was a year younger than her. I found out they had been friends since grade school, so why should I be too young?

I started my freshman year at the local high school. We had to ride this bus to school and it was intimidating to me because the boys on the bus were cruel and would shout out names, so I stayed close to the bus driver.

My sister always sat with her boyfriend, which left me alone. I did not go to school some days because of the teasing and mom not doing anything about it. She would just say ignore them. That was too hard of a thing to do. I would feel ill every morning before that bus but knew if I just waited and walked the long walk to school I would be okay.

I had my eyes out for a boyfriend this year but not any boys on that bus, thank you. I was a thin girl with long blonde hair and I loved to wear mini skirts. The school didn't like the skirts and would say something to me about wearing them so I started wearing tights underneath and they were satisfied with this. Girls where not aloud to wear slacks to school back then, and the coolest thing out in 1967 outside of the mini skirt were the cool hip hugger bell-bottom pants. I had one pair that was see threw material that I found out brought much attention from the boys.

I really didn't care much for school and I was absent a lot and my Step Father and Mother were not happy with me. I had very low self-esteem and didn't feel I could do well in school anyway. I had to put up with the boys on the bus teasing me and, My mother always telling me I was stupid and would not amount to anything, mostly when she was mad at me for something. I learned to believe her that I was stupid and it showed in my grades.

There was a career day at school and I was interested in Nursing but I believed what mom told me and was convinced I could not go for higher education. So I enjoyed the volunteer work at the nursing home near by along with taking a home nursing course in high school.

I loved to have slumber parties and have all my girlfriends over to stay up all night and talk about boys, and wearing our cute baby doll pajamas. We had a great time talking, giggling and trying not to wake my parents.

We tried a game of ESP and we had a crystal ball and would try to call up the dead. Weird things had happened during this time in this old 1900's house and I was not aware we were messing with the occult. Truly against God's word and what I was taught.

PART TWO

In the middle of my freshman year I met a boy named Tom, Short for Thomas. We both saw each other but were afraid to meet. I guess we were both a bit shy and I fifteen now just didn't know how to go about this thing. I asked my girlfriend Debbie to introduce him to me, as I was most excited to meet him, so that was the beginning of our relationship. I had no idea what was in store for me many years down the road. I was in love for the first time and I felt as though it was love at first sight. Matthew 26:41 Watch and pray, that ye enter not into temptation: the spirit indeed is willing, but the flesh is weak.

By the time I had turned sixteen, Tom had bought me an engagement ring that I found out came from a Pawnshop downtown. I thought maybe because he was low on money with no job but His parents said, "This would never last". They did not want him to invest a lot of money in the ring. I myself thought it was beautiful and I made sure everyone of my friends saw it especially Rhoda.

My parents said nothing because they did not know even though I wore the ring proudly. I felt this was the beginning of a real fairy tale, so I introduced Tom to my parents, but I noticed the look of disapproval on their faces. Tom even brought up the subject of wanting to marry me. My Father gave us the run down on the responsibilities of marriage and how we were too young to be thinking about such a thing.

Tom was not employed and Father brought this point up and said "You can't live off welfare." He was also adamant about a continued education. Father was a college graduate, so he felt that we should be thinking of this first. After Tom left I got a big lecture that this boy was not for me, he was all-wrong for me.

I became very annoyed because I had plans to marry him someday. My parents told me that I could not see this young man again. How dare they tell me this? I was engaged to him, and I was going to see him or else. I had no intent now to tell them I was wearing his ring.

I have no idea why they never questioned the ring cause I wore it everyday. I did like jewelry though, so maybe they saw it and thought I bought it for myself because I had my own money to spend as I pleased.

PART THREE

Later on I got my drivers license and had not said anything more to my parents about Tom, but I was still seeing him in secret. I would make up lies about where I was going and my friends would cover for me too. My sister would cover for me just as I did for her to see her boyfriend when she was not supposed to be seeing him.

I taught my sister some bad things, like how to slide out a narrow window of the second floor to the porch roof and down to the porch railing to the ground. This is how we would sneak out after dark on foot. I don't remember how we reversed the process but I must have been some climber.

I worked as a volunteer at the nursing home near by because I loved the thought of Nursing and caring for the elderly. Tom would come out to the nursing home and we saw each other frequently this way during my breaks.

As time went on things got more complicated in my relationship because Tom was asking me for sex; He just kept asking and asking. He even started to explain how you have sex, as I was never told these things.
I was so naïve and had lived a protected life.
He even told me about how to have oral sex with him, which I had not heard of before.

Everthing I ever knew came from medical books I read and became very interested in them.
There were plenty of them in the house library because my stepsister's brother who died left behind the books he had for medical school. I loved to read them, and also study anatomy and was or thought I was ready for sex.

Tom would ask me to go all the way like most guys did. For a long time I kept saying No! I knew the consequences could be a baby. My mother had always said if I had a baby out of wedlock I would be sent away and would have to give up the baby. I did not want that to happen to me so Tom promised me he would use protection. He always told me that he loved me very much and if I loved him I would consent to sex. Does that sound like most guys, they think with their body parts and not with their head?

I was reminded over and over that if I loved him I would go all the way with him. Like I said things were beginning to get complicated.

I was brought up in the church and I knew all the verses that said no fornication that was no sex outside the bounds of marriage. Why I had not been listening to God in these days of my life I do not know. I did know that not listening to God was going to cause me great sorrow that was to come. I was still a virgin and mom had never taken the time to talk girl talk. Only thing she ever said to me was stay away from boys. Or when you get married you'll wish there was a hole in the wall. She never told me why she said these things. She didn't even talk to me about a women's menstrual cycle, I learned that from a book also.

Mom had a real negative attitude towards sex. I had heard her say that her and my stepfather could not have relations together. They were going to counseling weekly for this. My mom and stepfather were carrying a lot of baggage from their former marriages which both ended in the spouse passing away.

PART FOUR

I continued to see Tom and I would try to call him and he was always out with the boys; his mother would be sure to let me know this. I suppose she got tired of me calling.

Tom and I went to school together and that was the time we made plans and would get together to see each other. Tom was a senior and myself now a sophomore.

We both took off for lunch one day off the school grounds. We had talked more about becoming sexually active, and this was the day. I told him it was a graduation present from me. I had really flipped out this time, gone over the far end.

It happened so fast at my former sister-in-laws house with no one around that there was no time for protection. Passion got in the way. I forgot that on your first time you have a little blood and I did not have a change of clothes for going back to school.

He was so gentle with me though and kind that I felt so safe in his arms and thought no more about the blood or getting pregnant. We both returned to school but who could think about schoolwork after this.

After my first experience in love making, it became a habit and a nightly affair. I was wrapped up in this new experience. We would meet and go out to the country where I learned to have sex in tight places and on the run.

I had told the neighbor lady next door about being sexually active with Tom as she was in her twenty's with two little girls, and I trusted her.

She started to let Tom and I come over. I would tell my parents I was going to see Frances at her house and visit. She would give Tom and I the guest bedroom and tell us to have fun. I think back and don't know how I did such a thing in someone's home with them knowing what was going on. What could I have been thinking about? In Gods word it is called Lustfulness, fornication.

Part Five

Tom had some friends and they would run around together and I was not invited. I just thought I had my girl friends and he had his boy friends. So I saw nothing wrong with this. Yet I was jealous when Tom would go to Zachary's house and I was told to stay away from there.

One day I could not find Tom anywhere and I did not like this. So I decided to go check Zachary's home to see if Tom was there. Zachary opened the door and I asked if Tom was there. "Sure he is here" then he let me in the door. I called for Tom and Zachary laughed and said, "There is no one home.

He forced me up the stairs to a room I guess it was his. He told me I would perform oral sex on him or else. I refused, so he tore off my pants and I struggled with him till he smacked me down on the bed and he commenced to rape me as I was screaming and fighting. When he finished he called me a Bitch and said get out of here. I got dressed and left but was too afraid of telling my parents because I was sure they would not believe me and say it was my fault.

I did tell Tom the next time I saw him and he said, "I told you to stay away from there!" I began to cry as he pushed me away. I expected him to comfort me and go tell Zachary off. Again like several times no one had used a condom.

I was so lucky not to get pregnant. In those days that was about the only fear there was for girls from not using protection. Had not heard of AIDS yet but was aware of other sexually transmitted diseases. But of course Tom would not have any of these. Right? He was a nice young man with a nice family.

PART SIX

Soon Tom Joined the service and I was at the end of my junior year. I really did not want him to go but I had no choice but to watch him become a man. This was his decision to join the service yet I don't remember him discussing it with me.

We spent the night together at my former sister-in-laws the night before he was to leave. It was so hard to let him go, knowing he would be gone for a year or so.

This started a very lonely period for me. Tom was stationed in a remote base in Alaska where they were indoors for an entire year.
It was too cold to go outside their buildings because they were in the most northern part of Alaska. It was a base with all men so they saw no women for over a year. We wrote back and forth with pictures for the whole time. I even sent reel-to-reel tapes and he did too.

By this time I was sharing with my parents that Tom was serving his country. I also told them I was getting mail from him at another address. My parents didn't say a lot about that, He was far away from me and I guess they were not concerned about a lasting relationship by mail.

Tom was so lucky to not have been sent to Viet Nam as so many were during this time. This was where his brother served. There was so much misunderstanding about this war.

Part Seven

In the spring of 1970 my love sent a letter to gain permission from my Father and Mother for my hand in marriage. I was now eighteen and I guess they knew that with or without their permission I was at the legal age to marry without a parents consent.

They did give me advice and asked was I sure that this was what I wanted as I had not really dated a lot of guys. I assured them that this was my dream so they gave Tom their blessing.

Soon my Sister and I started to plan my wedding. I started paying for the wedding myself, then my sister bought me my wedding gown and a set of stainless steel cookware. She was working at General Motors and made good money. Then mom decided to pay for the caterer, which saved me some more money. The date was up in the air yet. Tom was to get out in August of 1970 for a Three-week leave, but had not received his papers to say when.

Leah and I got everything done and we were ready to send out invitations because we finally got a time and date. I made it August the 22nd at 1:30pm of 1970.
My family went on vacation right before the wedding. I did not want to take the trip with my family to California. I was afraid I would miss Tom's first day back home.

Mom made arrangements for me to stay with her friend till her return; I guess she didn't trust me to be alone at the house. Besides our house was built in the 1900's and it was big and spooky to be alone in, especially in the black of night.

I had started back into the church since Tom left and had asked God for forgiveness as a fornicator. 1st John 1:9 "If we confess our sins, he is faithful and just to forgive us our sins, and to cleanse us from all unrighteousness."

When Tom got back to Indiana, I told him no sex till we were married. I explained that I had given my heart to God. He also said that he had asked

God into his heart and was a Christian also. He said that in the service before you marry that they counsel with you before you make the decision to marry. I thought everything was going so well. I was going to have a Christian husband and we would be going to church and all would be great.

Proverbs 27 says. Boast not thyself of tomorrow, for thou knowest not what a day may bring forth. Amen to that.

PART EIGHT

It finally came the wedding day, but I was a little concerned when I was told Tom had not arrived yet as I was finishing up the last touches. I guess he was just on time to enter with the groomsmen to the front of the church. So the wedding began with my Step Father on my arm for support and to give me away. The colors of the wedding were turquoise and white. Tom wore his military best. The church was full and I was ready but scared. One thing bothered me during the wedding and that was Tom hardly looked at me during the vows. After the reception and opening the gifts we went on our honeymoon at the lake cottage that his family owned in North Webster, Indiana.

We consummated our marriage that night and it was even more beautiful than before. I was so in love and was sure this was going to be just like a fairy tale. Living happily ever after. He was careful to fulfill every need sexually before he thought of himself. So there were no quickies. I was in heaven.

On the next day I awoke and Tom was gone. The car was there but he was nowhere to be found. I waited a long time and was very upset. Where could he be especially on our honeymoon? He finally got back and said, "He was no where." I just asked, "Then why could I not find you? He had no answer and I did not want to make things uncomfortable on our honeymoon. So I went about my business and fixed us up a meal on the hot coals of the grill. He always reassured me he loved me no matter what we were doing.

The next morning it happened again. This time I wanted a real answer to where he was going. He just said "Around". These are such vague answers. I tried to just let it pass as thought he might be having second thoughts or just worrying about his next service place to go. Maybe he just didn't want to talk about what was bothering him.

PART NINE

After the honeymoon we went to my mothers and packed our things in a small U-Haul trailer. The next day was the day to leave; Tom had to report to an eastern coastal state.

Tom had a nearly new 1967 Oldsmobile 442 that he bought from his brother that was in Viet Nam. We hooked her up to the U-Haul and told everyone good-bye with Mom crying of course. I had not ever been out of Indiana before so I started to cry too. We pulled out and I thought about leaving my family and starting a new life in a place so far away from everyone I knew. No more slumber parties., Giggling in the nights and telling stories. I had a new friend that was to be my life partner and my love. I cried off and on till we arrived to our new destination on the oceanfront.

Tom had to report in and get me signed up as his wife so I had an ID to get on to the base. Tom and I rode about the base getting acquainted where everything was. This was going to be a big experience for me. I had never had to cook out side of using the grill on the honeymoon. Grocery shopping was just a job mom did. So I had many new things to learn, but felt ready to take it on.

The first night we stayed in a small hotel south of the base. When Tom went to get a room I felt so embarrassed thinking that they might not think I was old enough or married since I was only 18.

I got over that once we got to our room. The place was not very fancy as we were limited on money but that didn't seem to matter much.

The next day we drove up and down the main drag and I saw the ocean for the first time. With all the new things to see and do I was feeling better. A first taste of being on my own.

We found us a temporary place to live at which was a hotel efficiency apartment on the ocean. You could hear the ocean waves and the seagulls. It was such a pleasant sound. But beside our kitchen window only a few feet away was a roller coaster ride and we were on the down side of the drop off and you could hear people screaming all night on the weekends. I finally learned to ignore that. I only had to walk out the front door to walk on the shore after I crossed the street. It was so peaceful out by the water and I collected lots of shells and sharks teeth to pass the time away while Tom was at the base.

Well a few weeks had gone by and I was learning the duties of a wife and the Military Base rules for a wife. Like don't go in certain buildings like the officer's club. I made that mistake and got into trouble. Tom and I would go to the base church together. I thought this was great. Didn't know anyone but, God was there and so was God's presents.

I decided I wanted a baby. As a young lady I wanted a baby for all the wrong reasons. I wanted someone to keep me company while my husband was on the base.

We talked about it and Tom was not ready and I begged him till he gave in.
We had a great time working on this baby. I didn't know there were so many different positions. In time I went to the base hospital and was tested positive to be pregnant. I was so excited yet didn't realize the responsibility of becoming a mother. I started shopping for baby things but found out that this town was not a baby or maternity friendly place.

I had to travel to a bigger city inland to find these things. I got a check from the service as Tom's wife so I started a checking account and was learning well how to use it.

At Thanksgiving time I became very sick with my pregnancy, but Tom had decided to go to North Carolina to visit a friend that he knew well from Alaska. Tom knew I was sick and still was going to go. I could not believe he would leave me here alone so far away from family to go see this guy in North Carolina. I don't recall how long he was gone but it was too long. I remember lying on the couch watching the Macy's day parade alone. And wishing I had someone to care for me. I started to feel a bit home sick.

Evening came and I was scared of the owner of the motel here as, He was such a real flirt. So I got a butcher knife and jammed it between the door trim and the door to prevent him from coming in with a key. I was for sure he might try this. Remember I have never stayed alone with no one to call if I felt threaten.

How dare Tom leave me in this condition? I felt confused and scared, what happened to love and care for in sickness and in health? When Tom did come home he brought the guy back with him. He was staying in the spare bedroom. I tolerated this but I was glad when his friend went back home.

Part Ten

Tom and I finally moved out to a duplex four blocks from the Ocean on Hollywood Drive. You could still hear the ocean waves with the windows open and smell the sea air and watch the fog roll in at night.

Down the road was an old graveyard that looked like something out of a horror movie. The grand oaks stood tall all around and the moss hug low and thick. With the fog added to this and the gravestones all crooked it was a bit spooky. We went there because of an old tale told about a women that died and never was married and it was told if you walked around her grave and held out a wedding ring she would grab it. Boo! I wasn't about to test her but the tracks around her grave told the story well enough for me.

It finally came time for the baby to be born. It was in the hot summer time. We had no idea back then what sex it would be though Tom was hoping for a boy like most men do. Tom took me to the base hospital and he had to wait in a waiting room. I found out I had to do this thing alone with strangers that were so military. The nurse was so stern and did not want to hear a peep out of me. She started to shave me with this straight razor and I thought I was going to loose it. Wait, "This is my first baby." I had not done this before and was lost to what was going on.

No one told you much of anything they just gave you orders. I had the baby natural and I had no idea it was going to be such a painful experience and they didn't teach you how to breath back then.

Well her name was Lynn. Reddish blonde hair 7 pound 9 ounces and a beautiful face.
I was in a ward of 8 women all older than myself. I watched them go home one by one till I was the only one left. After four days I finally got to take Lynn home. Tom asked me to drive home so he could hold her; I was not supposed to be driving so soon. She was wrapped up in a swaddling blanket nice and tight and was wearing the outfit that mom bought. I was so proud and so was daddy as he gave out cigars.

14

In the next day or so my mother flew down to help me with the bundle of joy. We had to travel a ways to get to an airport. After mother arrived she would bath Lynn for me and take care of the umbilical cord. Good thing she was there for I would have been last and scarred. She did this like old hat; she had not forgot her skills.

Tom was late getting home at nights and then he said they had drills that he had to be on base for the weekend and I could not call him. I just took him for what he said and went on with my life. Besides I had company with mom there.

Soon my Brother Terry came down with my niece Misty. She was always my little girl growing up and I don't think she quite knew how to handle all my attention going to another little girl. She looked so lost sitting on the porch. I'll never forget that look.

Life went on after the family left. I kept in touch with them my mail. Boy I wish we had e-mail back then, as it would have made things easier and I could have felt closer to my family up north.

Tom, Lynn and I became a little family of our own. Lynn kept me company and busy. There were lots of times Tom was late or not at home. He said it was all Military business.

Lynn started to grow and crawl and talk. She had the cutest little southern ascent. We would go on my bike down the street to the beach and play in the water waiting for Tom to get home. In January of 1973 Tom got papers for early out of the service. What great news, we were going back home to Indiana. After the moving van packed us up. We got in our car and headed up the highway ourselves.

Part Eleven

We arrived in Central Indiana where we called home. We stayed with my mom at first while looking for a home. Our belongings had arrived and were filling my mothers living room up. She did not use this room anyway so it did not cause problems for her.

After a week or so my Mom confronted me when Tom was upstairs in my old room. She said, "I have seen Tom's car at a well know gay persons house." "I think he may be Gay too." I was in shock and so mad at her that I told Tom what she said. He cried a minute and said "Don't do this to me." Well I did not know what I was doing to him then he told me that he had been accused of being queer since he was young. I felt bad for him, as I had never seen a man cry before so I went back to my mother and told her that she hurt Tom's feelings.

Soon after all that, we bought a home of our own. It was a brick colonel with two bedrooms and a fenced back yard, how perfect for my little family. The grade school was only one block from the house and there was a park not much further.

What mom had said that day back at her house always stuck in the back of my head but I was not going to believe such an accusation. How could I accept this?

This was my first denial for what was to come. John 8:32 "And ye shall know the truth, and the truth shall make you free".

My best friend lived not far away and she had had a baby the same year as me. So we got together as couples frequently till her husband moved them to Florida. Just when I was starting to get back to my roots and enjoy my best friend.

Tom did not wish for me to work and wanted me to stay at home so I did. I had no car and I had to bicycle if Lynn and I got out. I had a baby seat on the back and she loved to ride. The park was close by so we would go there to

16

swing and slide. Tom always had the car and came and went as he pleased. We were stuck at home except for the bike or mom coming by to take us out somewhere. If Tom took us with him he would tell me to wait in the car while he was in visiting whom ever.

Also he always had to leave in a hurry and this made it difficult with a small child and all the things they need before you go out some place. I was not always able to be ready in time to get to go with him and this upset me. Why could he not give us time to join him?

PART TWELVE

In 1976 I had my second girl and her name was Ellen as perfect as the first. On this trip to have a baby my labor was induced and I got to have Tom in the delivery with me and Mom was waiting close by.

Tom cried real big tears the moment Ellen was born. I asked him why he was crying and he just shook his head. On the way to my room Mom was waiting to see her new grand daughter.

I chose to have Ellen room with me, instead of the nursery. I spent about four days in the hospital but Tom did not come up to visit much till it was time to go home. I could not understand why he was not there every day but he said he had to work late and just went home cause he was tired.

Tom had a good job at a local Factory that made Fire Engines. He was a sheet metal man. He used to talk about a man at the factory that they called Paula, behind his back but was really Paul. He told me about things the workers did to each other that sounded really bad. I could not understand why they did these things to each other. Maybe it was a guy thing.

Soon Tom started working nights. I hated that with two little ones and me at home alone at night. He would get home late from work at times and he had no excuse except had to work over. I never saw his pay stubs to see if he really did.

I just felt that something just was not right but denied myself to go for mom's idea. It must just be me. I must be making something out of nothing. I was a real worry wart.

PART THIRTEEN

Tom became the President of the factories union then he started to go on weekend trips for the union and I could not understand why we could not go. He had a whole room cause he said he would be by himself, and we could enjoy the pool or shop or something fun.

A few weeks after returning home I noticed he had something wrong with his male organs. His scrotum was all swollen up on one side, really huge. He also had purulent drainage coming from his penis. He said with concern in his voice. "I have no idea what this could be." I suggested he get to a doctor soon.

He went to the Doctor alone and just said that the Doctor gave him a shot of penicillin for an infection. No more was said. Some time after this cleared up I kept coming up with vaginal infections. I was treated several Times and he had to be treated also. Things were going along pretty good after all this, and we would visit with family and go on family outings together. Tom always called me beautiful and said he loved me.

PART FOURTEEN

Then another surprise came.
Next it was Lice! No not just any lice but crab lice. I started to think about what my mother had told me some years ago a bit more seriously.

Could this be true is my husband Gay? He said he got the lice from a public restroom. I really did not buy that especially with him treating his problem himself and I guess trying to keep it a secret. He was not going to vounteer any information everything was all right; I was just getting myself upset over nothing.

He took me to bed one night and wanted to make love I looked into his face which at this time he had a beard and mustache. I saw these bugs in his beard and then I saw them on his pubic hairs. I was shocked but at the same time mad. We both had to be treated this time to get rid of these crab lice. Needless to say, there was no sex that night.

How sickening this was, there was infidelity going on and he worked hard to try to keep me happy and do what ever he possibly had to do to get me to forget what happened. Tom always got me to believe it was not his fault. And I was always in denial so life went on. I promised to love him for better or worse. I was keeping my promise even though it hurt. I was also to embarrassed to let my family know I was having problems. I don't even think I told my best friend Rhoda.

Over and over Tom would be gone and have a stupid excuse. I would be upset and then there would be a honeymoon period. Only to follow again with his absents. I knew there was something very wrong in our marriage but I could not put my finger on it and did not want to believe my mothers opinion.

Next Tom got the news that the factory was closing down its doors after 104 years. I was scared for us and General motors was not hiring anymore. They were even cutting back and this was what kept the town together.

There just were no good jobs. Tom finally got a job in construction that he worked at for awhile. We were doing okay on this salary. But again he was gone a lot. One night he did not come home. I sat up all night as I had made a special dinner and candlelight and the girls were with grandma.

Tom was on the CB radio frequently and his handle was minuteman. I heard a few people laugh in the back ground when I would be trying to get a hold of him. They would comment it only takes him a minute all right.

He continued to be gone all night and we were having a terrible blizzard. They had told people to stay off the streets and I had no idea what happened to him. Morning came and I was scared and crying that something awful had happened to him.

It was near Christmas time, and when he got home he gave me a ridiculous reasons to why he was late. He told me how he left to go to circle city to go shopping for something special for me for Christmas. Then on the way home he came upon a stranded motorist that was stuck in the tall snow and helped him out.

Tom had no packages to show for his time. I was upset with him, So there was another honeymoon period and convincing me that I was imagining things again that he loved me so much and never wanted me to leave him. I was finally convinced that it was all me not him that was the problem.

Later that morning he went to bed. I stayed up in a chair and felt I was in a catatonic state. I had a knife in my pocket I was obsessed with using it on him or me. I did not know then that mental illness was in my family. I can somewhat remember the kids coming in without grandma and asking what was wrong with me. I can't even remember answering them. I had to have sometime as I got up and fixed a meal cause I remember all of us at the table and no one saying a word, especially not me. Then somewhere along the line I snapped out of it and came to my senses.

Part Fifteen

Time went on and he started telling me he was going to see his mom and I was always told to stay at home. Time would go by and I would call his moms and he had never been there. When he would get home I would ask him how his visit was and he would tell me great. I knew he was lying now to me and trying to cover up something, someone, but I had not a clue yet.

Colossians 3:9 Lie not one to another, seeing that ye have put off the old man with his deeds.

Since the factory closed down, Tom had to find another job other than the construction job, as he didn't keep that busy. His Brother had a growing company in Florida and offered a job to work for him.

Florida right where my best friend had moved. I was tickled. Mother and I took Tom to the airport to get to Florida and I stayed home to sale the house. Thank God it sold in three months.

We lived in this home in Indiana from 1973 till 1979. We had put a lot of money in the home to make it better. It had an all-new kitchen with appliances and new wall-to-wall carpet throughout the deep thick kind.
It was so nice and we also made a good profit.

The Girls and I were going to join Tom now and the moving van came and moved our things. We got to Florida before the moving van brought our belongings. And we were living in a small duplex again. So much different than having one's own home.

I could not get used to the looks of Florida. I would ask myself what I was doing here. The homes were made of block and stucco not much style to them. Then Tom told me that we were going to build a home. I could not believe what I was hearing. I had never been in a new home and now I was going to live in one. Tom promised that things would be different down here.

See his Brother had a Construction company and Tom worked for his brother so we could save by doing a lot of work ourselves. That in it's self saved us so much money. We had found the perfect lot before building started. I saw it in a dream and I recognized it. I said, "That's it." That's the one. Tom bought the lot and the house was finished after 3 months.

Oh I forgot to tell you that when we first got here and lived in the duplex, that his brothers office was close to the duplex where we lived and Tom would say he had to do some work at the office and I would feel bad for him and the girls and I would walk down there to feed him, and get there and he would not be there nor was anyone else. Clue! Things have not changed.

PART SIXTEEN

We found a church after the house was finished and Tom said that everything was going to be different from now on. I wanted to believe him but I was always suspicious. Tom did go to church with the girls and me and I was glad to have him by my side. He asked the pastor to dedicate our home to the Lord so he did that for us.

After getting into the new house I had to take a job so I worked in a daycare so my youngest not attending school could remain with me. I was the type that wanted to raise my own children and not give them to a sitter or care center while I worked. So this job made it possible for Ellen to remain close to me.

My brother that moved down just as we had moved into our new home brought his family with him and moved in too. A brand new house with pale blue carpets and my brother got a greasy job and it was not long till I could see road tracks on the carpet.

The first new home in my life and I had never been in a new home and this was happening. I complained and soon my brother moved out and in his own place which was good cause his stepdaughter and my girls would fight.

PART SEVENTEEN

As soon as both daughters were in school I got to drive our car. Remember we only had one car but Tom was driving the company truck. Then his brother said that he saw the truck where it did not belong and did not look good for his Christian company and had to let Tom go.

Tom had come home late and said he was let go because his brother was down sizing the company. I already knew he had lied. I tried to keep the tears back and decided that I had to get a job that I could make a living with if need be. My mother always told me I was stupid and would not amount to anything but I was out to prove her wrong this time I was desperate.

I had always been interested in medical books and so I chose nursing school. With the girls in school I was able to go to school myself.

We were short on money and I went to Sunday school and there was an envelope on my seat. I opened it and it said that my books and supplies for nursing school were paid for. I never knew who did this. I then was granted a scholarship. God was looking out for the girls and I. I prayed so hard to get this dream. I worked hard in school and I graduated with perfect attendance, which was a first for me, and I had A-B grades. I was determined I was going to be a good nurse as it had been my dream from a little girl.

Mom came down to visit and see our new home. She was proud of me for graduating and with perfect attendance and good grades. She came to the graduation ceremony and I felt good about myself for once. A few months later I went to take state boards. I passed with flying colors. I was now an LPN.

PART EIGHTEEN

I got my first job at one of the local hospitals in town. It was the first place I went for an interview and they started me out on nights. You had to work there a while to get a day shift.

I would get off work take the girls to school and then sleep a while and then go pick them up and fix dinner and sleep a while longer.

I was working on an orthopedic wing. I had a great charge nurse and she was a great teacher. I worked for 5 years and then was offered a job on days for they were opening a new unit. I went to special training for telemetry reading and working with the critical patient. I was oriented in the ICU for three months. I was the only LPN working in this unit. We had four patients a piece. Most of them where on life support and very ill needing much attention. I was proud to be on this floor as it added meaning to my life.

Went to church on Sunday morning and the pastor of the church wanted to speak to Tom. I found him and gave him the message and he refused to go see him. That was a red flag.

I went to the pastor myself several days past and asked what it was he wanted to speak to Tom about? He asked if I really wanted to Know and I said I think I already did know, with tears in my eyes and my hands clinched tight.

I waited to see what he had to say to me hoping it was not what I was expecting.

The pastor sat down and began to tell me about a man in the church that confided in him that he was having sex with other men and my husband was also doing this. I heard what I expected but I was not as prepared for it as I thought. I had been lying to myself all these years, not really wanting know the truth.

Tom gave me an excuse when I told him where I had been and why. He said the other man did not know what he was talking about. That he must have him confused with someone else.

One day I was going to the store in the car, I parked and noticed something under my seat so I reached down to investigate. "Oh my Lord" I thought with disbelief "It's gay pornography" I was shocked at what I saw. I quickly put it back under the seat and asked myself "What Now?" When I got home I got that trash out of the car and filed it away for proof. I had been praying for God to show me the truth and God was opening my eyes.

I did not want to accept what my mother tried to tell me in 1973. I was even trying to ignore God's signs. It was now 1996. I had two older daughters now and things were getting more complicated. I was so upset that I had to take medical leave. I called a crisis line and they told me they could help me and made arrangement for an airline ticket.

PART NINETEEN

That evening I told Tom I was leaving for California a while to think about our marriage, and I guess he didn't believe what I was saying. Up to now he had always been able to say he was sorry and make me believe things would be okay. I told him about the plane tickets and he reluctantly took me to the airport. We said very few words on the way. He kissed me and said he loved me so much. I said "good bye" and I got on my TWA flight.

The flight was long and I was so confused. I was leaving everyone and would be alone in a strange place. I did not tell my family in Indiana as I did not want them to know what I had been going threw.

My mother was gone now. She died of cancer in 1986. I'll never be able to tell her "I'm sorry I did not listen to you." "You were right"!

I was so young, when mom said she suspected Tom was gay. I thought she was making trouble so she could have her little girl back.

Mother knew early in my marriage, and if I had of investigated it instead of trying to avoid finding out the possible truth, I would have been saved many years of emotional turmoil. I was too afraid of the truth.

I still was not facing the truth even with many other witnesses, and all damaging material I had found and hid. I did not want to believe the man I married was a person I did not even know.

Part Twenty

I arrived in L.A. and I saw a young man holding a sign with my name. I went to him to make sure it was I he was looking for. He helped me into the van and we traveled down the fast freeway across town. I had never been in such a big place as this in my life. I just took it all in with Tom in the back of my mind as I cried.

We arrived to this small hospital not even thinking about it being a mental hospital. I had been so disturbed and shocked I just wanted a safe place to stay and think. I just could not stop crying.

I checked into the hospital here in California and I filled out the admission papers and they led me down a long hall and the door locked behind me. I was led to my room where they took my hair dryer, razors, and string from my shoes. Anything else they felt you could harm yourself with, but I did not have any thoughts like that only shock, despair and disbelief. How do you compete against a man? I knew how to compete against another women. I was grieving.

We had meeting all day at this nice place with nice people with their own set of problems. I felt alone with my problem. No one in the world could be going through what I was going through. We were given a Bible and reference book and a test to take with all kinds of questions about you, mood, feeling and so forth. I was being evaluated for my mental health.

I didn't talk to anyone unless they spoke to me, because I just would start crying again.

After a day I tried to call Tom. I got no answer. I tried again and told him that the counselors wanted to have a conference call with us, but Tom said there was nothing to talk about and hung up. I cried again as he was in denial big time. I did not call him back or any one in my family. I was too ashamed to tell them what was going on.

After many days went by I was feeling a little better and they talked to me on a daily bases. After a few weeks they made sure I was ready to go home before they would get me a flight home. I was going home but what was ahead?

I flew into Fort Myers airport and Tom was there with kisses and hugs and a limo and roses with a bottle of Champaign. I knew this was another peace offering to get me to forget and have things back to normal. The honeymoon period.

I said very little and was cold toward Tom and did not know what I wanted to do. I felt trapped. I still knew I loved him and could not imagine being with out him in my life. Then there were the girls. How could I break up a marriage and take away their dad. Oh. So much to think on.

We got home and there was silence. I then got the pornographic book out that I had found in his car. He said it did not belong to him. I told him "I found it in your car!" "Someone must have put it there." He replied.

He then continued to make me feel I was wrong and he was right and lets get on with life.

In the mean time there was a park in town where gay men hooked up with one another. The bad thing was that this one guy was a serial killer. I guess he hated gay men and would get to know them and take them away from the park. Kill them and cut their heads off and other body parts and bury them in different places around town. I told Tom." You could have been one of those men that were killed. He said nothing for a minute. Then he said, "Everything is over and things will be okay."

I soon told my daughters about things going on and they said very little. I don't think they could believe what I was saying either.

Some weeks after this my daughter saw her dad's van at the park. She reported to me she saw her dads van when driving by the park. When Tom got home I questioned him about it and said, "Your daughter saw your van at the park". He said, "I was there to use the restrooms". "I had to go really bad". I bet he had to use the rest rooms.
On the same note he hugged me and kissed me and told me not to get upset." I was getting upset over nothing." See a peace offering again. When is the honeymoon?
Proverbs 25:19 Confidence in an unfaithful man in time of trouble is like a broken tooth, and a foot out of joint.

Part Twenty-one

I tried to get Tom to go to counseling he was stern with me and said "I did not trust him. Well Duh!

Things were very stressful at work and I didn't need more stress. Then a letter came in the mail to Tom and I didn't recognize the name or address. I opened it up and was shocked to find a note from a gay man that wanted to get together the next time he was in town. Said he "Enjoyed their last visit. That the last man he was with just rolled over and went to sleep. Of course, Tom denied knowing this person. Even though it had his name and address on the front. Again he sweet talked me and buttered me up and took the letter and threw it in the trash upset. Then he took off mad in the van and didn't come home for a while.

When he left I took the letter out of the trash and put it with the book he denied having and filed them away.

Tom had screwed up my head again and had me believing everything was okay. I still tried to get him to go to counseling and he continued to refuse stating it was not necessary for him. "You go."

Time went by and I tried to forget all that had happened in the past years and decided we could be friends and just live together. There was not anything sexual going on between us anyway at this stage.

Tom had been working for a golf course and that didn't last long. Then he worked for a local retail store and someone must have had it out for him. They did a number of things to his car but the worse was when someone removed all the lug nuts from the wheel and the tire flew off and caused an accident.

Since then Tom had changed jobs twice from two golf courses to working with two guys that lived in a city about 50 mile south of us. Here he did landscaping and I finally got to meet the guys he worked for and guess what. Yes, they were gay buddies. I did not like this situation. Tom would go early and have breakfast with them and stay after work to have a drink and snack. What an arrangement. Wonders what else they did?

PART TWENTY-TWO

One day Tom went to donate blood. I don't know why but he did. Another week went by and the County Health department called to tell him his blood showed Syphilis. They made him an appointment and he went in not telling me about this. But surprise!

They had to notify those he had been in sexual contact with. Or should I say the county does that. So I was notified and asked to come in to see them. The questions they ask where humiliating. Like how many sex partners do you have? One. Do you have same sex Partners? No. Do you use Protection? No. I don't have sex cause my husband said there is no reason for condoms.

The health department told me I should use protection no matter what. Tom got a shot and they gave me one and tested me for Syphilis, but I was free of the disease. I also had them do an HIV that was negative also.

God was protecting me. And I was getting all kinds of signs of outside sexual activity. Tom had no way of getting out of these lies any more. I got brave and asked Tom about his sexual life outside of our marriage.

I told him to talk or I would walk! Was this coming out of my mouth? The one that has always been quiet to keep the peace. Hurting inside and crying alone. Denying and lying to myself for fear of the truth.

Tom was not getting out of it this time. There was silence as I sat there in tears. I said, "Look at me". He started to tell me how he had been with men and had been having sex with them since about 14 years of age. I asked him if he had been molested at a young age. He said, he could not remember.

I had heard stories of a certain family member that had committed incest. I asked him did this person rape him. He still had no recollection. I asked him if he was the giver or receiver of the contacts, he said "The giver."

I was shocked to what I was hearing, but relieved it was not my imagination. All his contacts were casual sex no steady person per his words. No protection was used and he was coming home to me all these years and not loving me enough to care whether he or I got a STD. How could someone tell you all their life, they loved you more than anything and do this? That's why in 1973 he said "Don't do this to me" He did not want to have to confess then.

He did not want to confess now but he was afraid of me leaving.
He continued to tell me he was not bisexual nor was he gay. So what was he?

He said, "He loved me very much and did not want to lose me." I was living in his closet. Who would suspect a married man with children to be gay? But it is happening in large numbers right now. It is estimated that over 4 million women are married or have been married to gay men and in almost all cases, unknowingly.

Tom began to tell me that all his contacts have been casual sex, hundreds of men. No protection had been used. I guess he is immune to getting a sexually transmitted disease. Not! I know that from the past years. I believe he was in denial about that too.

There are several support groups and books out there to help the straight spouse.

PART TWENTY-THREE

I had heard enough. I had to be at work in the morning and I was an emotional wreck. No one to talk to because he was in the closet and I was protecting him. I could not sleep all the night and I began to think the only way out would be to take my life. I was not thinking straight at all. I had been in denial and depression for so long I was starting to show mental breakdown.

I went to work the next morning and I could not control my crying. I could not function. If someone said something I only cried more.

The hospital found me a replacement and I then was called into the office and sent to the mental health office of the hospital.
I remember talking to them telling them my husband was gay and I was dismayed. I remember taking things from my locker after I talked to their counselors still crying. I have no idea how I even got home.

I remember nothing else. I don't even remember how I become unemployed. I guess I had a nervous breakdown.
I do know I took an overdose of drugs. I called some crises line and they called 911 because I was so lethargic and I had told them I took an overdose. I was Baker acted meaning you are a threat to yourself or others.

The ambulance came and was loading me up just as my husband arrived home. I have no idea what was going through his mind but they told him what I had done. I bet he didn't tell them who caused me to get so extreme with my emotions.

I was monitored closely at the mental hospital, but Tom did not come in to see me. I was in a lock up unit with no communication with the outside world. Broken and feeling like my husband had just died. I tried to stop crying. I asked to see the Pastoral care. He prayed with me and with his soft word I felt comfort to my emotion turmoil. I was assigned a psychiatrist and he put me on medication.

I was diagnosed with Depression, Bi-Polar disorder, and Anxiety and Obsessive-compulsive disorder and posttraumatic stress disorder. Now I really felt like I was the problem.

I was in and out of the hospital ten times that year 1999. All for attempted suicide. My mind was sick, shocked and not functioning. Tom had hurt me bad. All those years gone by and my husband were having his addictions of lust with men he did not know.

Again and again he apologized and tried to smooth things over. He was going to take me to church and be a good husband.
He always treated me well except for not caring what disease he might get and pass onto me unknowingly.

Tom is a leader in the community and if this got out I'm sure he would not be. I don't want to destroy his being in the community. I just want him to quit this behavior. He says it's over now, But as always there is that mistrust.

Always wondering what will happen next. I have asked God for strength to Love him and forgive him. I'm still under a Doctors care and have to see a counselor every two weeks. I have good weeks and bad weeks and still have to go to the hospital at times for my safety. Tom wants me to forgive and forget.

I also lost my Job and I'm on Disability. The Finances really dropped and we had to spend three years in bankruptcy. We don't have sexual relations anymore. One reason is he refuses to wear protection. So I have to protect myself. He really doesn't show any attraction to me for sexual contact anyway. I feel cheated. I feel as if I am just living with a companion. I looked to the Internet to see if I could find anything on my problem. I just knew I was the only one going through this kind of thing.

To my amazement I found I was not alone anymore. I found a chat line with the str8's1 found on Yahoo.com It was a good thing. I could talk to others now and found out their stories were similar to mine.

They had meeting here in Florida and other places in the USA. We would get together and tell our stories. It is a way to make contact with others like you. We were like a family. Lots of hugs which I needed and above all the support. There were also men that discovered lesbian wives coming out
To find it search under Straight Spouses of Gay Men. Or try www.Gayhusbands.com

Then I found a chat line of other wives of gay husbands and I chat on Sundays and Thursdays on an AOL chat line. You would not believe the similar stories I have heard.

Part Twenty-Four

It's now 2005. My grown daughters know about their father, and they still love him. He is their father and my husband I promised to marry for better or worse. I am praying daily to be a godly wife and have the strength to endure. Some days it is difficult for me. Especially if I let my thoughts get the best of me when I suspect him cheating on me, or he is gone a little too long.

1 Corinthians 7:13-15 and the women who hath a husband that believeth not, and if he is pleased to dwell with her, let her not leave him. For the unbelieving husband is sanctified by the wife, and the unbelieving wife is sanctified by the husband: else were your children unclean; but now are they holy. But if the unbelieving depart, let him depart. A brother or a sister is not under bondage in such cases: but God hath called us to peace.

Tom wishes to remain with me. I'm Living Inside His Closet everyday, but maybe we can both come out someday. Proverbs 3:5-6 Trust in the Lord with all thine heart; and lean not unto thine own understanding. In all thy ways acknowledge him, and he shall direct thy paths.
No matter what happens we will remain the closest of friends, Augie

OTHER BOOKS

The Other Side of the Closet by Amity Pierce Buxton, Ph.D.

On the Down Low by J.L.King

Steps out of Homosexuality by Frank Worthen

Coming out of homosexuality by Bob Davies and Lori Rentzel

Someone I love is Gay by Anita Worthen and Bob Davies

Uncommon Lives: Gay men Straight Women by Catherine Whitney

Husband Who Love Men by Aileen Atwood, RN Ed. D

Straight Spouses, Gay Men By John Malone

Gay Husbands/Straight wives: A mutation of Life, Bonnie Kaye M. Ed

Is He Straight? A checklist for women that wonder. Bonnie Kaye M. Ed

HELP GROUPS

Love In Action International Inc.
 4780 Yale Road
 Memphis, TN 38128
 (901)751-2468

Straight Spouse Network (SSN)
 Amity Pierce Buxton PH. D
 8215 Terrace Drive
 El Cerrito, CA, 94530-30
 (510)525-0200

Gay Husbands/Straight Wives
 www.Gayhusbands.com
 By Bonnie Kaye M. Ed.

Myself Augie Mikesell
 Gustalynn@yahoo.com

ABOUT THE AUTHOR

Augie lived a pretty normal child hood having one older brother and one younger brother and a stepsister. Cared for by a nanny till age 14 when my mother remarried and started a new life. I live with my husband in a companionship relationship. We have hobbies and enjoy them together. I have 2 daughters ages 29 and 34. I also have 3 grandchildren; two are age 6 and one age 12. We love family gatherings and having the kids over. I Love to have out of town family stay with me and spend time together.

I also have 2 son-in-laws that my daughters love.

I am under medical care for a number of illnesses and on disability. I do what I can and wanted to be sure and share my story in a tactful way to protect those involved. When you love someone you want to protect him or her. I want to live my life to be a good example of a person that loves God and family. I hope you enjoy my book. And again thank you Rhoda and Colette who encouraged me even though I still hear my mother call me stupid. I have come a long way with love and patients. I still had to go through some rough times to get to this point. I have a special sister-in law that listens to me daily whether I am depressed or in a good mood. I am working at being more positive and helping people in their troubles and taking my mind off me. The Joy of the Lord is my Strength. God is my helper in all things. Romans 8:23 "And we know that all things work together for good to them that love God, to them who are called according to His purpose."

978-0-595-37096-2
0-595-37096-9

www.ingramcontent.com/pod-product-compliance
Lightning Source LLC
Chambersburg PA
CBHW050344290526
45785CB00006B/2633